OUR SOUTHERN NEIGHBOR
MEXICO

THE PACIFIC NORTH STATES OF MEXICO

JANET BURT

UNITED STATES

Tijuana

Mexicali

32°N

Nogáles

Agua Prieta

30°N

BAJA
CALIFORNIA

Isla
Angela de
la Guarda

SONORA

Hermosillo

Isla
Cedros

28°N

Isla
Tiburón

Ciudad Obregón

MEXICO

Gulf of California

BAJA CALIFORNIA

Rio Bravo del Norte

26°N

Isla
Carmen

Los Mochis

BAJA
CALIFORNIA
SUR

Isla Magdalena

Isla San José

Isla Espíritu Santo

Culiacán

Isla Cerralvo

SINALOA

N

24°N

Isla Santa
Margarita

W   E

La Paz

S

PACIFIC OCEAN

Mazatlán

22°N

Cabo San Lucas

NAYARIT

0   100   200 Miles

Islas
Marías

Tepic

0   100   200 Kilometers
Albers Conic Equal-Area Projection

116°W   114°W   112°W   110°W   108°W   106°W   104°W

OUR
SOUTHERN NEIGHBOR
MEXICO

THE PACIFIC NORTH STATES OF MEXICO

JANET BURT

Mason Crest Publishers
Philadelphia

Mason Crest Publishers
370 Reed Road
Broomall PA 19008
www.masoncrest.com

First printing

1 3 5 7 9 8 6 4 2

Library of Congress Cataloging-in-Publication Data on file at the Library of Congress

ISBN 1-59084-089-5

TABLE OF CONTENTS

OUR SOUTHERN NEIGHBOR MEXICO

Roger E. Hernández
Senior Consulting Editor

INTRODUCTION

exico is a country in the midst of great change. And what happens in Mexico will have an important impact on the United States, its neighbor to the north.

These changes are being put in place by President Vicente Fox, who was elected in 2000. For the previous 71 years, power had been held by presidents from one single party, known in Spanish as *Partido Revolucionario Institucional* (Institutional Revolutionary Party, or PRI). Some of those presidents have been accused of corruption. President Fox, from a different party called *Partido de Acción Nacional* (National Action Party, or PAN), says he wants to eliminate that corruption. He also wants to have a friendlier relationship with the United States, and for American businesses to increase trade with Mexico. That will create more jobs, he says, and decrease poverty—which in turn will mean fewer Mexicans will find themselves forced to emigrate in search of a better life.

But it would be wrong to think of Mexico as nothing more than a poor country. Mexico has given the world some of its greatest artists and writers. Carlos Fuentes is considered one of the greatest living novelists, and poet-essayist Octavio Paz was awarded the Nobel Prize for Literature in 1990, the most prestigious honor a writer can win. Painters such as Diego Rivera and José Clemente Orozco specialized in murals, huge paintings done on walls that tell of the history of the nation. Another famous Mexican painter, Rufino Tamayo, blended the "cubist" style of modern European painters like Picasso with native folk themes.

Tamayo's paintings in many ways symbolize what Mexico is: A blend of the culture of Europe (more specifically, its Spanish version) and the indigenous cultures that predated the arrival of Columbus.

Those cultures were thriving even 3,000 years ago, when the Olmec people built imposing monuments that survive to this day in what are now the states of Tabasco and Veracruz. Later and further to the south in the Yucatán Peninsula, the Maya civilization flourished. They constructed cities in the midst of the jungle, complete with huge temples, courts in which ball games were played, and highly accurate calendars intricately carved in stone pillars. For some mysterious reason, the Mayans abandoned most of these great centers 1,100 years ago.

The Toltecs, in central Mexico, were the next major civilization. They were followed by the Aztecs. It was the Aztecs who built the city of Tenochitlán in the middle of a lake in what is now Mexico City, with long causeways connecting it to the mainland. By the early 1500s it was one of the largest cities anywhere, with perhaps 200,000 inhabitants.

Then the Spanish came. In 1519, twenty-seven years after Columbus arrived in the Americas, Hernán Cortés landed in Yucatán with just 600 soldiers plus a few cannons and horses. They marched inland, gaining allies as they went along among indigenous peoples who resented being ruled by the Aztecs. Within two years Cortés and the Spaniards ruled Mexico. They had conquered the Aztec Empire and devastated their great capital.

It was in that destruction that modern Mexico was born. The influence of the Aztecs and other indigenous people did not disappear even though untold numbers were killed. But neither can Mexico be recognized today without the Spanish influence.

Spain ruled for three centuries. Then in 1810 Mexicans began a struggle for independence from colonial Spain, much like the United States had fought for its own independence from Great Britain. In 1821 Mexico finally became an independent nation.

The newly born republic faced many difficulties. There was much poverty, especially among descendants of indigenous peoples; most of the wealth and political power was in the hands of a small elite of Spanish ancestry. To make things worse, Mexico lost almost half of its territory to the United States in a war that lasted from 1846 to 1848. Many still resent the loss of territory, which accounts for lingering anti-American sentiments among some Mexicans. The country was later occupied by France, but under national hero Benito Juárez Mexico regained its independence in 1867.

The next turning point in Mexican history came in 1911, when a revolution meant to help the millions of Mexicans stuck in poverty began against dictator Porfirio Díaz. There was violence and fighting until 1929, when Plutarco Elías Calles founded what was to become the *Partido Revolucionario Institucional*. It brought stability as well as economic progress. Yet millions of Mexicans remained in poverty, and as time went on PRI rulers became increasingly corrupt.

It was the desire of the people of Mexico to trust someone other than the candidate of PRI that resulted in the election of Fox. And so this nation of more than 100 million, with its ancient heritage, its diverse mestizo culture, its grinding poverty, and its glorious arts, stands on the brink of a new era. Modern Mexico is seeking a place as the leader of all Latin America, an ally of the United States, and an important voice in global politics. For that to happen, Mexico must narrow the gap between the rich and poor and bring more people in the middle class. It will be interesting to watch as Fox and the Mexican people work to bring their country into the first rank of nations.

Mountain peaks rise above the landscape in Baja California. The states of Mexico's Pacific North region—Baja California, Baja California Sur, Sonora, Sinaloa, and Nayarit—feature a wide range of terrains, from dry desert to beautiful coastal beaches and fertile valleys.

1

THE LAND

The northwest corner of Mexico has some of the most fascinating geography found on the continent. The states of Baja California, Baja California Sur, Sonora, Sinaloa, and Nayarit form the Pacific North region of Mexico, and these states contain a wide variety of landforms and climates. Wild, untamed mountain ranges, miles of *arid*, barren desert, beautiful inviting beaches, volcanic terrain, and fertile valleys are all found in this region. It is a land of contrast where startling differences exist side by side. The geographic features of the area, formed before the coming of modern human civilization, have not been tamed by progress. Instead, progress has attempted to adapt to the ancient, timeless terrain of the Pacific North region of Mexico.

Baja California is the most western part of this region, a large peninsula that stretches south for 800 narrow miles (1287 kilometers). It lies between the Pacific Ocean and the Gulf of California, which is also called the Sea of Cortez. The *inlets*, *lagoons*, and twists and turns of the land give Baja more than 2,000 miles (3,225 kilometers) of coastline. Many of the beautiful beaches, however, cannot be easily reached. In many instances, a four-wheel drive vehicle is needed. And in spite of this large coastline area, most of the Baja Peninsula is dry, hot, and rocky.

The peninsula of Baja is divided into two states, Baja California Norte, also called simply Baja California, and Baja California Sur. The 26,997 square miles (almost 70,000 square kilometers) of Baja California Norte occupy the northern half of the peninsula. The American states of California and Arizona border Baja to the north. The capital of the state, Mexicali, is located near this border. The Mexican state of Sonora is the boundary for the northeast corner of Baja California. Sonora is the only land contact between the peninsula and the country of Mexico, but Sonora is connected to Baja California by a stretch of barren desert. The Gulf of California to the east and the Pacific Ocean to the west provide the boundaries that create the peninsula. This also isolates the peninsula from the rest of Mexico. To the south, Baja California Sur edges Baja California.

Baja California Sur has 27,571 square miles (71,409 square kilometers) of territory, with Baja California providing its only land boundary. The capital city is La Paz, located at the southeast end of the peninsula. It connects to mainland Mexico by ferry across the Gulf of California. Like its northern neighbor, Baja California Sur is a rugged land full of contrast. It has beaches, deserts, mountains and, in the central section, volcanoes.

Common geographical features bond the two states on the Baja Peninsula. Tall wild mountain ranges run through the center of the Baja like a backbone. These mountains begin in Baja California with the Sierra De Juarez, which are near the U.S. border, and these regions are much the same as they were hundreds of years ago. The Sierra de San Pedro Martir mountain range rises further south. The highest peak

Signs of ancient cultures are common throughout Mexico, from temples and cities to carvings, handcrafts, and sculpture. These ancient paintings were found in a cave in Baja California Sur.

on the Baja, Picacho del Diablo, is found in this range, rising to a height of 10,073 feet (3,070 meters). This mountain range contains plant life that is found nowhere else in Mexico, and it provides a home to several **endangered** species. A small range, the Sierra de San Francisco, is further south. The Sierra de la Giganta continues this spine of ranges into the south, with the Sierra de Laguna finishing at the southern tip of Baja California Sur.

This long chain of mountains adds to the wildness and isolation of the Baja Peninsula. Not only is the entire peninsula isolated from the rest of Mexico by the Gulf of California, but the interior parts of the Baja are separated from each other by the rugged mountain ranges. These mountains are places of wonder and mystery. **Petroglyphs** dating from the earliest people to live in this area have been found in the caves. In the Sierra de San Francisco, near the town of San Ignacio, cave paintings cover a large part of canyon walls. These are dated from 100 B.C. to A.D. 1300. These paintings can only be accessed by

Cacti choke the ground in the Pinacate Desert. Although the hot, arid climate is not good for growing many crops, certain plants thrive under the conditions.

horseback (or muleback); there are no roads leading into this wilderness. The Sierra de Juarez to the north also has cave paintings.

These rough mountain ranges rise from the desert. In fact, much of the Baja Peninsula is desert. The climate is hot, burning and dry. During some years, it does not rain at all in parts of the Baja Peninsula. The desert is not a friendly place unless you are a cactus, a reptile, or some very adaptive plant life. Baja's central desert is under protection because of the kinds of plants that live there, since this is the only place in the world where some of them can be found. The world's largest cactus, the giant cordon, which can be 60 feet tall, grows here. A special plant called the boojum has learned how to protect itself in this harsh environment by growing straight up in a spire shape. It does not get branches until it is at least 100 years old, and it grows only about one foot every 10 years. Some of these plants are 500 years old. The soil is very thin in this desert, and only odd and determined groups of plant life can grow there.

The desert stretching the length of the eastern Baja creates the threads that weave Baja California with Sonora, its neighboring

Mexican state. Sonora is 70,484 square miles (182,553 square kilometers) and the second-largest Mexican state. Hermosillo is its capital. Baja California borders Sonora on the northwest. The United States borders it on the north, and the Gulf of California makes the western boundary. The state of Sinaloa forms the southern border, and the Mexican state of Chihuahua is the eastern border.

The landscape of Sonora is much like the Baja, except that it has a large coastal region on the west. It also has mountainous areas in the Sierra Madre Occidental. There are four rivers that run east to west: the Alta, the Sonora, the Mayo, and the Yaqui.

It is the desert that Sonora shares with the Baja that is its major landscape. This is the third largest desert in North America. Most of the area is harsh and lonesome. This Region of the Gran Desierto looks barren with its layers of endless sand dunes. However, despite the 100-degree temperatures (38 degrees Celsius) every day for three months at a time, more kinds of cactus, other plants, and animal varieties live here than in any other North American desert.

The Pinacate Biosphere borders this desolate dune landscape. This is a park that is a field of volcanic craters. It is close in distance to the U.S.-Mexican border but worlds away in appearance. The largest crater is El Elegante. It has a diameter of 4,600 feet (1,402 meters) and is about 500 feet (152 meters) deep. There are many other smaller craters in this park, formed from multiple volcanic eruptions that happened millions of years ago. Even though this park has a blackened landscape from the volcanic ash and in the summer temperatures can reach 200 degrees Fahrenheit (93 degrees Celsius), some wildlife and desert cactus thrive here. Humans do not live here but many visit and climb the crater to experience this timeless environment.

The Sonoran Desert does have a pattern of rainfall, which helps the growth of some plant life. The saguaro cactus is the symbol of this desert. The cactus has fruit, which can be eaten, grows 50 feet (15 meters) tall, and can live as long as 200 years. The saguaro cactus has a flower that blooms at night, and this gives the desert bats nourishment. In turn, the bats pollinate new cactus. A full-grown saguaro cactus can weigh eight tons.

The desert stretches south toward the border of Sinaloa, a long and narrow state that has 22,521 square miles (58,329 square kilometers). Sinaloa is sandwiched between the Gulf of California and the foothills of the Sierra Madre Occidental. Sonora borders it on the north. Chihuahua and Durango are the Mexican states that form the eastern border. To the west is the Gulf of California and Nayarit is to the south. The capital city is Culiacan.

The geography keeps the same general features as the rest of the Pacific North but with some changes. Sinaloa has four main rivers. The largest river is the Fuerte, followed, north to south, by the Sinaloa, the Mocorito, and the Piaxtla. These rivers run down from the Sierra Madre Occidental toward the Gulf of California. While there is still desert in parts of Sinaloa, Sinaloa contains more surface water. There are fertile valleys, jungles, mountain forests and thick vegetation. With the help of *irrigation* projects, it has become a productive agricultural area for Mexico. Areas on the coast such as Los Mochis are irrigated and lush with mangoes and acres of flowers. The coast itself has beaches, islands, and lagoons.

A lone flower pokes through the cooled rocks of a basalt flow in the Pinacate Biosphere Reserve in Sonora. Mexico is home to many active and inactive volcanoes, and the residue of their eruptions is evident across the land.

Nayarit, the southern border of Sinaloa, is the smallest state in this region with 10,547 square miles (27,317 square kilometers). Durango and Sinaloa border it on the north, with the state of Jalisco on the east and south and the Pacific Ocean on the west. Nayarit's geography reflects parts of all of the other Pacific North states. It has scrubby, dry areas along with the mountains that are part of the Sierra Madre Occidental. However, there are also fertile areas with abundant rain. Nayarit also has two volcanoes: Ceboruco and Sanganguey. Ceboruco last erupted in 1879. The areas surrounding the volcano are covered in red lava. This makes the landscape starkly beautiful.

These states reflect the best that Mexico has to offer. Nature has been untouched in many areas. The waters of the Pacific and the Gulf are clear and teeming with fish. Inland the mountains offer rocky challenges and breathtaking landscapes. Freshwater rivers run through fertile valleys. The desert flows through the states with shimmering heat and exotic plant life. The Pacific North states are a geographical mosaic of space, openness, and contrast.

THE PACIFIC NORTH STATES OF MEXICO

BAJA CALIFORNIA NORTE

Location: The United States to the north; state of Sonora on the northeast corner; Gulf of California to the east and the Pacific Ocean to the west; Baja California Sur to the south

Capital: Mexicali

Total area: 26,997 sq. mi. (69,922 sq. km.)

Climate: Hot, dry.

Terrain: Mountainous.

Elevation: Below sea level (Mexicali) to 10,000 ft.

Natural hazards: Tsunamis; earthquakes; some hurricanes.

BAJA CALIFORNIA SUR

Location: Baja California Norte to the north; Gulf of California to the east and the Pacific Ocean to the west

Capital: La Paz

Total area: 27,571 sq. mi. (71,409 sq. km.)

Climate: Hot, dry.

Terrain: Mountainous.

Elevation: Sea level to 10,073 ft. (highest peak).

Natural hazards: Some hurricanes, volcanoes.

SONORA

Location: Baja California to the northwest; the United States to the north; the Gulf of California to the west; the state of Sinaloa to the south; and the state of Chihuahua to the east

Capital: Hermosillo

Total area: 70,484 sq. mi. (182,554 sq. km.)

Climate: Hot, dry.

Terrain: Mountainous.

Elevation: Sea level to 10,000 ft.

NAYARIT

Location: States of Durango and Sinaloa to the north; Jalisco on the east and south; Pacific Ocean to the west

Capital: Tepic

Total area: 10,547sq. mi. (27,317 sq. km.)

Climate: Hot, dry, some areas have rain.

Terrain: Coastal plains; hilly inland.

Elevation: Mostly sea level; inland regions as high as 10,000 ft.

Natural hazards: Volcanoes.

SINALOA

Location: Sonora to the south; Gulf of California to the west; states of Chihuahua and Durango to the east; Nayarit to the south

Capital: Culiacan

Total area: 22,521 sq. mi. (58,329 sq. km.)

Climate: Hot,dry, some areas have rain.

Terrain: Coastal plains; mountainous inland; river valleys.

Elevation: Mostly sea level, but some mountains up to 10,000 ft.

2

THE HISTORY

The history of the Pacific North region reflects the same theme as its geography, for its wild, isolated populations are different from the rest of Mexico. Isolation has kept progress at bay and has shrouded the history of this area in mystery.

Most of the southern and eastern areas of Mexico have evidence of ancient sophisticated Indian populations, large groups of people who had a highly organized civilization—but this is not true of the Pacific North region. There is definitely evidence of early human occupancy with tools and artifacts dating from A.D. 1100, but none of the huge pyramids or artistry that reflect an advanced culture are found here. Instead, wild tribes like the Chichimecas were scattered across this land. These groups were *nomads* who also wandered into the southern portions of Mexico. The geography of the Pacific North area did not encourage building and permanent settlements.

These Cora Indians are taking part in a religious festival. Their religion includes both Christian and pagan elements, and they protect its secrets fiercely.

When the Spanish entered Baja California in 1534 they found the Cochimi Indian group, a tribe that is thought to date back 14,000 years. The Cochimi lived by fishing and gathering fruit and seeds. They left behind cave art that can still be seen today.

In Baja California Sur, the Guaicuri (pronounced *waikuri*) Indians were the main tribe. There were several thousand members of this group, but they were primitive. Life on the Baja was harsh, and their main concern was survival. They did not build buildings for dwellings but took shelter where they could find it. Constantly on the move, they hunted whatever was available in the mountainous area. There is little known about the organization of their society.

Across the Gulf of California in what is now the state of Nayarit, the Cora Indians did have a tribal structure. These were a fierce tribe who lived in the mountain ranges of the Sierra Madre Occidental. Like the mountains they lived in, the Coras would not be easily conquered. While the Spanish claimed these lands in the 1500s, they did not send colonies of settlers to live there, and when they finally did begin to colonize this land, the Coras resisted with violence. In the early 1700s the Spanish sent a large military force to deal with the Coras, but the Coras still would not submit to the Spanish way of life. Those who survived the Spanish military ran to the mountains. The few Indians that were captured refused to become Christians.

The Yaqui was another tribe of this region. Their main base was along the Yaqui River in Sonora. They had some agricultural skills and grew beans and corn. However, hunting and gathering wild plants was still a main source of food for them. Like the other Indians in this

These bells are important to the Yaqui Indians of Sonora. They are used not only for funerals but for happy occasions as well, to accompany music, dancing, and celebration.

region, they lived in scattered groups and did not, at first, have a formal government. When the Spanish arrived in the 1500s, the Yaqui defeated them. However, by the 1600s the Yaqui made a treaty with the Spanish. The Spanish gave the Yaqui livestock animals and taught them more about farming. The Yaqui prospered, and over the next 100 years, the Yaqui stayed in towns and had a form of government. The Spanish used them as skilled laborers and mine workers. By the 1700s, however, the Yaqui wanted more freedom than the Spanish system provided, and they rebelled. Unfortunately, during this rebellion they lost the prosperity they had gained. The Yaqui were forced to flee to other parts of Mexico and to the United States.

A Seri Indian woman sports a traditional Mexican head wrap. Many of the native people of Mexico continue to live according to cultural conventions.

Another fierce tribe that lived in this region was the Seri. The largest settlement of Seri was the Isle de Tiburon (Shark Island), a large island in the Gulf of California off the Sonora coastline. Though the Seri did travel the Sonora Desert, the island was their main *habitat*. Like the other tribes of this region, the Seri hunted for their food, but they were also fishermen and expert boat makers. They made boats out of reed that were sturdy enough to survive the shark-infested waters between the Isle de Tiburon and mainland Sonora. In these waters they hunted giant sea turtles with *ironwood* spears. Even though freshwater streams were on the island, there was not much open land that could be used to grow crops. So the Seri were also nomads. They crossed the Gulf in their reed boats and moved to the interior of Sonora in constant search for game and wild plant life.

The Seri Indian group was small, with only about 5,000 people when the Spanish arrived. The Seri resisted when the Spanish tried to convert them to Christianity and turn them into a farming people. This resistance led to their near extinction. In the 1600s, several hundred Seri living on mainland Sonora rebelled against the Spanish. The Seri did not stop fighting until every adult Seri was killed. The Spanish sent the surviving children to **missions** scattered throughout Mexico, but war between the Spanish settlers and the Seri went on for another two centuries. Some of the Seri tried to settle down and live on the missions, but they could not tolerate the confinement. When they attempted to leave the mission, they were hunted down, and the women were separated from the men and sent to Guatemala. The Seri still did not submit. They raided neighboring settlements and completely destroyed the mission at Guaymas. The Spanish then forced them to retreat farther and farther into the desolate country. Disease and starvation took many lives. By the 19th century, the Seri were reduced to only 500 people. However, these 500 have kept their cultural identity, and the Seri still exist as a people in Mexico today.

The Spanish conquerors were not able to colonize the Pacific North region of Mexico the way they did the rest of Mexico. At first, settlers tried to colonize the Baja because of the pearls that were to be found in its sea, but the attempt failed. When silver was discovered in what is now Sinaloa, this again brought settlers—but it also brought conflict with the Indians. Between the harsh climate and the violent reception from the native people, only small, isolated pockets of Spanish settlement stayed in this region. The Spanish set up Nueva Viscaya, a governing area for these settlements. Present-day Sonora and Sinaloa were included in this, while present-day Nayarit was included in an area called Nueva Galicia. Nueva Galicia and Nueva Viscaya were eventually combined and renamed Sonora y Sinaloa. The settlement was left to the missionaries, but the Jesuits were expelled in 1767. The Franciscan monks remained, however, and Spanish settlers began to increase. The Spanish took tribal lands, and constant conflict was the result. The Spaniards controlled the region until 1821, when Mexico won its independence.

The Native Americans did not take part in the politics of Mexico or the revolutions that shaped the nation in the 19th century. When the 1910 revolution took place, however, one of the leaders was Alvaro Obregon from the Pacific North region. He organized the local Indians to help the president, Francisco Madero, stop the rebellion. Alvaro Obregon became president in 1920, and he established educational reforms.

Dollars also began to flow into the northern border area because of the *prohibition* laws in the United States. These laws made it illegal to sell alcohol, so many Americans came to Mexico to buy what they could not buy in the United States.

The next president, Plutarco Elias Calles, also came from Sonora. He tried to reform the agricultural system. During his presidency, the Partido Nacional Revolucionario (PNR) was formed. This was the beginning of a political party that still exists today, although it is now called the PRI. Not everyone agreed with the ideas of President Plutarco Elias Calles, and fighting broke out. Much of the conflict was about who owned the land.

Francisco Madero is credited with starting the Mexican Revolution in 1910 after a fraudulent election. His actions helped remove Porfirio Díaz from power. Afterward, Madero was elected to the presidency.

In the 1930s an *ejido system* helped create peace within the country. This gave community land to the local farmers. The politics of the 1940s and 1950s helped the Pacific North region. Dams were built that made cultivation possible in the area. Large irrigation projects opened new possibilities in this area. In the 1960s, economic help for the region arrived in a different form when the Border Industrialization Program began. This was the beginning of the *maquiladoras*, the assembly plants that would provide much needed jobs. With the jobs, however, came a different lifestyle for the natives of this area. Many factories today have unsafe conditions and unfair pay for the workers employed there. Around the world, there is growing concern about the big foreign companies who take advantage of the maquiladora system.

Vicente Fox, shown here on the campaign trail, was elected president of Mexico in 2000. His election ended the seven-decade dominance of the PRI political party in ruling Mexico.

A new political party, Politico de Acción Nacional (PAN), focused more on business than farming, and the people of the North Pacific region supported the new party. The country was surprised when, in

1989, Ernesto Ruffo, a member of PAN, won the governor's election in Baja California Norte. The mayors in Tijuana, Mexicali, in Baja Norte, and in Hermosillo, the capital of Sonora, were also PAN candidates.

In the year 2000, Vicente Fox Quesada was elected president of Mexico. In the past, every president of Mexico had been a PRI candidate. The PRI had held power for over 70 years—but Vicente Fox Quesada was a PAN candidate. His political ideas had been born in the north. He picked Ernesto Ruffo to assist him during his presidency.

The Pacific North region has finally overcome its isolation. It has now taken an important place in shaping the politics of the country. The region still faces many challenges that are tied to its geography. The majority of the people are settled in a few places, and this raises concerns about ecology and health. There are other challenges, such as the gap between the rich and the poor. However, the region has adapted to change in a way that preserves tradition but looks forward to progress.

A colonial stone building stands beside glass architecture in Mexico City. One of Mexico's most interesting traits is the juxtaposition of the ancient and the modern.

THE ECONOMY

The economy of the Pacific North states reflects the continuing growth and change in the region. Geography helped to shape the economy, since the region has trade borders with the United States. Also, minerals come from the mountain areas, while farms flourish in the fertile valleys, and tourists come for the beautiful beaches.

The North American Free Trade Agreement (NAFTA) is one of the key factors in the economic growth of Mexico. This is especially true of the Pacific North region. This agreement was negotiated between the United States, Mexico, and Canada in 1991, and it was completed in 1993 and became active on January 1, 1994. One goal of NAFTA is to remove trade restrictions between the countries over a 15-year time period. Import *duties* are abolished between participating countries. This means a country does not have to pay a tax to sell products from one country to another. The agreement brings Mexico into one of the largest trade zones in the world. NAFTA removes barriers and therefore speeds up the process of buying and selling. It provides more opportunities for investment and encourages cooperation between nations.

NAFTA is not the answer to all of the economic growth in Mexico, however. In some instances, in fact, it has created problems. In 1995, under President Zedillo, there was a financial crisis from an imbalance in trade. More money was going out of the country than was coming in. **Interest rates** went up and people were having a hard time paying for necessary items. By 1999, however, Mexico's economic situation had begun to improve.

Maquiladoras have created much of the growth. The maquiladoras are assembly plants where the pieces of a product are **imported** into Mexico without any tax. The product is assembled in Mexico. It is then **exported** from Mexico, again without paying a tax. U.S. businesses are attracted to Mexican maquiladoras because they do not have to obey American safety regulations or pay their workers as much as they would have to in the United States; this means the factory owners can make their products more cheaply. Despite the poor working conditions, and even though most of these plants or factories are owned by foreigners, they still boost the economy by providing jobs. This creates the need for more technology. More electricity, running water, housing, roads, and transportation are needed to support all of the people who are working in the maquiladoras.

The Pacific North region has felt the benefit from this system more than any other part of Mexico, since 35 percent of all of the Mexican maquiladoras are in the Baja Peninsula. People from all over Mexico travel to Baja California to find work. Tijuana, on the United States border, has the bulk of these assembly plants. It exports electronics, auto parts, textiles, and plastics. Tijuana is the number-one exporter of televisions in the world. Japan, the United States, and Spain all have major investments in both Baja California and Baja California Sur. Well known corporations such as Black and Decker, Casio, Matel, and Sony have large factories in Baja California. However, the working conditions in these factories are often poor, and the workers may receive as little as 75 cents an hour in American money.

Most of the growth in the Baja Peninsula is contained in the north. Baja California Sur has few maquiladoras and less foreign investment. Its major exports are salt, seafood, and textiles. The tourism industry is still developing.

Across the Gulf of California, Sonora, the second largest state in Mexico, is experiencing growth on a

A factory worker pours liquid into molds in a maquiladora in Tijuana, Baja California. The maquiladoras developed from a need for cheap labor and new trade agreements between the United States and Mexico.

**A farmer herds livestock on his ranch in Mexico.
For many families in the hills of Mexico, the old ways
still govern daily life.**

large scale. It, like Baja California, is geographically situated on the border of the United States. It is Mexico's leading producer of electronic equipment, plastics, and chemical products. Companies that invest in Sonora include Ford Motor Company, AT&T, Pepsico, and Velcro USA. Most of this production takes place in Hermisillo, the capital of Sonora. Hermosillo has made an effort to become a major industrial city. It was not as close to the border as some cities so the lure for the maquiladeros

A farmer turns his soil, cracked by a lingering drought.

was not as strong, but Hermosillo created an industrial park in an effort to draw the employment base farther south. Ford came for the industrial park, and the large baking company Sara Lee is in another industrial park. Everything that is needed for the business is in one place. The city of Guaymas is also experiencing growth. It has a deep-water port, and IBM and ITT Power Systems also have interests there.

Sonora has agricultural products as well, such as wheat, corn, and cattle. **_Reclamation_** projects on the Yaqui, Sonora, and Mayo Rivers have opened new agricultural areas. Cattle ranches are important to the economy, and pork is also a large industry, supplying 30 percent of Mexico's needs. Sonora also exports pork to Japan. Mining is

A commercial cruise ship prepares to dock on the Mexican coast. Tourists are welcomed on Mexico's Pacific coast, where they can cross the border from the United States for an affordable and exciting vacation.

another industry for Sonora. Copper, gold, and *graphite* are mined and exported.

South of Sonora, the state of Sinaloa relies more heavily on its natural wealth than Sonora. Agriculture thrives in its lush river valleys. The northern two-thirds of the state is rich in agricultural products. The state industry is based on the processing of the agricultural wealth. Cotton and sugarcane are two of the major products.

Sinaloa is a Mexican leader in agriculture, fishing, and aquaculture. It has the largest canning facility in Latin America. A part of its agriculture is beekeeping, which is a growing industry in Sinaloa. The beekeepers rent their hives to farmers for pollination purposes.

In spite of Nayarit's small size, it is one of the leading tobacco growers in Mexico. Seventy-five percent of tobacco production in the country happens here. This state also has more varieties of fruit than any other state. Exports include mangoes, wood, and coffee.

Tourism is common to all of the states of the Pacific North. Tourist activities vary from state to state. Nayarit, for example, is well known to bird watchers all over the world. Its unique marshes and forests attract a large and unusual variety of birds.

The economic picture for all the states in the region is one of growth. The years 2000 and 2001 were among the best ever for the region's economy.

BAJA CALIFORNIA

State GDP: 148,810,050 (in thousands of pesos)

Percent of GDP:
Manufacturing: 8%
Commerce: 48%
Services: 44%

Per Capital Income: 17,376 pesos

Exports: Electronics, auto parts, textiles, plastics

BAJA CALIFORNIA SUR

State GDP: 23,116,381 (in thousands of pesos)

Percent of GDP:
Manufacturing: 10%
Commerce: 51%
Services: 39

Per Capital Income: 17,504 pesos

Exports: Salt, seafood, textiles

Resources: The ocean

NAYARIT

State GDP: 23,368,891 (in thousands of pesos)

Percent of GDP:
Manufacturing: 10%
Commerce: 47%
Services: 43%

Per Capital Income: 8,758 pesos

Exports: Tobacco, mangoes and other fruit, wood, coffee

Resources: Farmland, forests

SINALOA

State GDP: 80,786,268
(in thousands of pesos)

Percent of GDP:
Manufacturing: 9%
Commerce: 49%
Services: 41%
Other: 1%

Per Capital Income: 11,070 pesos
Exports: Cotton, sugarcane

Resources: Farmland, ocean waters

SONORA

State GDP: 114,298,480
(in thousands of pesos)

Percent of GDP:
Manufacturing: 9%
Commerce: 43%
Services: 46%
Other: 2%

Per Capital Income: 17,583 pesos

Exports: Electronics, plastics, chemicals, pork

Resources: Copper, gold, graphite, farmland

PER CAPITA INCOME = the amount earned in an area divided by the total number of people living in that area
GDP = Gross Domestic Product, the total value of goods and services produced during the year
1 PESO = about $0.11(2003)

Figures from INEGI, the Mexican National Institute of Statistics, based on Mexico's 2000 census.

A bullfighter strides confidently towards his opponent. Bullfights are a popular sport in the Pacific states, particularly in Mazatlán.

THE CULTURE

The original population of this region was Indian. The Spanish arrived with Cortés, but some of the native groups managed to remain independent of the Spanish. They kept their heritage and language, and today these groups are small populations of Cochimi, Cora, Seri, Yaqui, and some smaller groups. For the most part, they have not joined Mexico's progress. They survive through farming and selling their art and crafts. They have kept their language and do not speak Spanish.

The **mestizo** population, however, speaks Spanish, and their primary religion is Catholicism. About five percent of the population follows traditional native religious beliefs.

The Indian people of this region value their community. They try to stay isolated from the rest of Mexico so they can keep their community together. Their traditions include religious rituals that have been handed down through the centuries, but Christianity has mixed with the traditional native religion. While Christianity is accepted, it is celebrated quite differently by these native people.

Each of the states in this region has its own personality. Most of the population clusters in the urban areas, with small farming areas in

42

the outlying regions. The Indian populations tend to live in the mountainous areas where they can avoid the bustle of the city life.

In Baja California, 90 percent of the state's population lives in the cities. It is a young state, with 78 percent of its population under the age of 40.

In this region the tradition of the bullfight has remained. When Spain ruled Mexico, people celebrated most holidays with bullfights, and today in Baja the bullfights take place on Sunday. The bullfight is an entire sequence of events that the people recognize. It opens with a person who asks formal permission to hold the fight. Then the bullfighter enters the arena. The assistants follow. When all of the participants are in place, a bull weighing up to 1200 pounds charges into the ring. The bullfighter does not challenge the bull yet, however. He waits and watches how the bull moves. The assistants then close in on the bull. They stab the bull in the back with long lances. When the bull begins to bleed, he shakes his head in rage. As he stomps and swerves, three pairs of barbed darts are stuck into his hump. The bullfighter then asks permission to kill the bull. He has to kill the bull within a certain amount of time or leave the ring in disgrace. This is when the bullfighter uses his cape to direct the bull's charges.

Mexico's ethnic groups
Indian-Spanish (mestizo): 60%
Indian: 30%
White: 9%
Other: 1%

Education **12 years of education is required from ages 6 through 18. About 94% of school-age children are enrolled in school. The literacy rate is 89%.**

Mexico's religions
Roman Catholic: 89%
Protestant: 6%
Other: 5%

A mariachi band begins to play during the seventh annual Mariachi Festival in Guadalajara. More than 40 mariachi bands gathered to play in an attempt to have the festival entered into the Guinness Book of World Records.

The bull follows the cape movement as the bullfighter gets closer and closer. Finally the bull drops his head lower and lower as he tires. The bullfighter then draws his sword and kills the bull. It is important that he kill the bull quickly and with one stab of the sword, since the swiftness of the kill is one of the ways a bullfighter is judged. While bullfighting is not a tradition in most countries, it has been a part of Mexican culture since the arrival of Cortés.

Traditions that have lasted for centuries are also reflected in Indian life in the Pacific North area. The Sonora Desert is the home of the saguaro cactus. In the past, this cactus helped sustain Indian life under harsh conditions. Today, the tradition of gathering fruit from this large cactus is still practiced.

In late June, family groups gather to collect the fruit from the cactus. This is a long process that involves the entire family. The family comes together and camps in the foothills at the edge of the desert. They get up just as the sun begins to rise. One or two people knock the cactus fruit to the ground with a long pole that is made

44

from cactus rib. Then the fruit is opened with a sharp knife. The skin is thrown aside and the fruit goes into the bucket. Once the buckets are filled, they are carried back to the camp, where the fruit is mixed in water. It sits for an hour until all of the rocks and sand particles fall to the bottom of the bucket. The top layer is then scooped out and heated on an open fire. Seeds and pulp are taken out of the mixture and set aside to be dried. The syrup is returned to the fire and cooked until it is the right consistency. During the hot, all-day process, stories are told and history is passed down from generation to generation.

The people of the Pacific North region are warm and friendly. They enjoy spending time with their families, and many family-oriented festivals take place throughout the region. Most of the festivals have fireworks, parades, and food. As in the rest of Mexico, the national holidays are celebrated, and March is Carnival season. This holiday is a celebration that takes place right before the

A man playing the role of Jesus Christ carries a cross through the streets of Iztapalapa during Holy Week festivities. Mexico is a primarily Catholic nation, and celebrations during the Easter and Christmas seasons are particularly passionate.

40 days of Christian **Lent**. It is a carnival complete with parades, floats, and street dancing. In the Pacific North, the port cities have extravagant celebrations and tourists are welcomed.

At the end of Lent is *Semana Santa* (Holy Week), a religious holiday that includes Good Friday and Easter Sunday.

Cinco de Mayo, or 5th of May, is another favorite national Mexican holiday. It celebrates the Mexican victory over the French army.

November 1 is the Day of the Dead in Mexico. This important holiday comes from the Indian culture. People bring flowers to the graves of dead relatives. They welcome the souls of the dead back once a year to visit their families. A festive meal is served at home, and just before midnight the families go to the cemetery with lighted candles to guide the souls of the dead back to their graves. People are silent as they think about their memories of the dead person.

Some of the **fiestas** are only celebrated in local areas. For instance,

* San Blas in Nayarit celebrates the blessing of the sea festival in February;

* in May, the Nayarit farmers celebrate Fiesta St. Isador when seeds, animals, and water are blessed;

* Mexican Navy Day is celebrated in Guaymas with a staged naval battle and fireworks;

* Baja honors its missionary history with the Día de Nuestra Señora, celebrating the first mission in Baja.

Some celebrations are new to the Pacific North region and are sponsored locally in an attempt to bring visitors to the area. An example

Papantla flyers peform for tourists in Mexico. The men wind rope around a high pole, tie it to their feet, and jump off, swinging in circles and unwinding the rope.

	STATE POPULATION	GROWTH RATE
Tabasco	1,891,829	2.4%
Baja California	2,487,367	4.2%
Baja California Sur	424,041	3%
Sonora	2,216,969	2%
Sinaloa	2,536,844	1.4%
Nayarit	920,185	1.1%

is the Festival Aeronautical held in Culiacan, Sinaloa. This was the first balloonist festival held here. It was a small beginning, but those who participated enjoyed the experience. The local people were enthusiastic and helpful, and the international participants formed bonds and left with good feelings. This may become an annual celebration.

All of the celebrations in Mexico involve music and dance. The music of Mexico reflects its people, for it is a blend of Indian and Spanish tradition. Drums, rattles, and flutes were in use before the Spanish arrived, and the Spanish brought stringed instruments. The Pacific North festivals usually include

Day of the Dead participants march in a parade to the town square in Mexico City. The festival celebrates the lives of the friends and family who died in the previous year.

lively music that calls to the people to enjoy the festivities. The native populations have retained some of their traditional dances. Folklore groups perform these on special occasions. For instance, the Sonora Yaqui perform the Stag Dance, celebrating the life and death of the deer, a primary food source for the tribe. The lead dancer wears a dear head while performing the dance. In Matzatlán, the dance of the *voladores* (the flyers) is performed mostly for visitors. The dancers climb a pole high in the air, then push themselves off and revolve 13 times until they reach the ground.

All of the dances, like the festivals, are celebrations that give the people of this region a chance to come together. Time spent with families, friends and community is important to the Mexican culture.

A cliff drops off into the the Sea of Cortez. Mexico's coast is dotted with white and red sand beaches, as well as cliffs and Mayan ruins.

THE CITIES AND COMMUNITIES

The communities and cities of the Pacific North region of Mexico vary in size. Each has its own unique atmosphere as well.

In Baja California these communities range from bustling, crowded urban centers to quiet, out-of-the-way villages. Mexicali, the capital of Baja California, has 700,000 residents. It is a modern city that began as a small village with less than 500 people. It grew steadily until the 1960s, and since then the population doubled and then doubled again. The areas to the south of Mexicali are irrigated valleys. Many varieties of agricultural products are grown there. Most of these products go through Mexicali to be distributed. Some of them are sent throughout Mexico and some of them are exported.

While Mexicali is a large business center, it is the city of Tijuana to the east that is better known. Due to its closeness to the U.S. border, large numbers of tourists go to Tijuana. The shopping is duty free, and products are imported from all over the world. In fact, the largest shopping center in northwest Mexico is in Tijuana. In addition to the shopping, nightlife in Tijuana offers a party atmosphere. Tijuana's nightclubs are open all night long, so this is not a place where people go to find peace and quiet. It is the fourth-largest city in Mexico, with over 1,000,000 people. The people who now live in Tijuana come from all over Mexico. Many of them come to use Tijuana as an entry point to the Unites States. They get jobs in the maquiladoras and decide to stay in Tijuana. There is not enough housing for many of the new arrivals, so houses are often built from whatever is available, including wooden packing crates and even cardboard boxes. Conditions are poor in many parts of the city. However, there is a strong belief that hard work will overcome difficulty. Those new to Tijuana have hope for a bright future.

South of Tijuana is Ensenada. This is not a small town, but it seems small in comparison to Tijuana. Ensenada is the biggest fishing port in Mexico and has about 370,000 people. It has **canneries** and is also the center of a wine-growing area. Ensenada promotes tourism to help its economy, and cruise ships use the port. The city is home to over 75 cultural and sporting events each year.

Guerro Negro is a town of 5,000 people just below the border of Baja California in Baja California Sur. It is a small but important place, with a special combination of desert and sea. The sun and ocean breezes dry the sea salt in large salt ponds. One third of the world's salt comes from this small place, but another natural happening makes this place important also. Each year between 10,000 and 20,000 gray whales come here. They travel 6,000 miles, **migrating** from Alaska to Guerro Negro's calm, warm lagoons. These whales come to play and give birth to their

50

Shoppers flock to the markets and stores in Tijuana. Mexico offers duty-free shopping, making prices much lower than in the United States. Vendors also present unique handcrafts made by Mexican folk artists.

young. Since this species is extinct in the North Atlantic, the Mexican people are protective of these whales. The adults can be 50 feet (15 meters) long and the calves are fifteen feet (4.5 meters) long. In order to protect the females, the males swim at the mouth of the lagoon, while the females and the calves stay toward the back of the lagoon. All sea and air traffic is stopped from nearing the lagoons during whale season so that the whales are not disturbed. Tourists who want to see the whales have to view them with binoculars.

La Paz, the capital of Baja California Sur, has almost 200,000 inhabitants. Its name means peace, but La Paz does not have a peaceful past. The community had to struggle to survive, since its isolation got in the way of successful colonization. A mission was started there in the 1700s, but when disease destroyed most of the Indian population, the mission disappeared. Pearls were found there in the 1800s, and a permanent settlement was started. Development stopped, however, when disease killed the oysters in the bay. Finally, the excellent sport fishing and the beautiful beaches began to draw

There are many vital ports along the Pacific North coast of Mexico. Living near the ocean has its advantages, such as better access to foreign trade as well as fishing.

tourists. Today, La Paz is home to the University of Baja Sur. Resorts attract commerce, and a ferry connects La Paz to mainland Mexico. The town stretches out along the largest bay on the Baja Peninsula. At long last, it lives up to its name, for it is a peaceful, family place.

Beautiful beaches also pull tourists 130 miles south to Cabo San Lucas. This town of 3,000 residents is set at the southern tip of the peninsula. Jesuit missionaries established a mission there in 1730, but floods and rebellion put an end to the mission, and in 1840 the site was abandoned to pirates. Today it is a mushrooming tourist location. Not only are the beaches lovely but excellent golf courses have been built that attract golfers from all over the world. Cabo San Lucas also has a busy nightlife, and clubs are open until the morning hours. Most of these clubs are located along one main street, and walking is the option chosen by most people.

Across the Gulf of California is Tepic, the capital of the state of Nayarit. Unlike Cabo San Lucas, Tepic does not attract swarms of tourists. It is an urban center with a population of 260,000. The atmosphere of

A native Mexican dives from a steep cliff in Acapulco. Water sports and adventure sports are popular throughout the country.

this city is welcoming and the people are known for their kindness. This city also has a low crime rate. In contrast to the modern city, the mountains that surround Tepic are wild and sparsely inhabited. The mountain residents, Cora and Hiuchol Native Americans, try to avoid the city. They want to keep their ancient culture intact. However, they do make their artwork available for purchase.

In the state of Sinaloa, north of Tepic, is Mazatlán. This city of 300,000 is Mexico's chief Pacific port, and the country's largest shrimp fleet docks here. The name comes from an Indian word that means "place of deer," but there is no evidence of deer in the city today. The large shrimp industry and agricultural production supports economic growth. The tourist industry thrives in an area apart from the production area. Baseball and bullfights are traditional pastimes of the residents and the tourists. In Mazatlán, the death-defying cliff divers also perform, diving from cliffs 45 to 50 feet above the water. Timing is extremely important

The city of Taxco boasts picturesque colonial buildings. The historical area is also conveniently close to silver mines and the scenic Cacahuamilpa Caves.

in this sport. Divers watch the waves and dive when the wave is in close to the shore. If they waves are out, just six feet of water and bone-crushing rocks await them at the bottom.

The capital of Sinaloa is Culiacan. Like Tepic, this city of 600,000 people is not a place that draws many tourists. Instead, it is a modern agricultural center. Archeological evidence indicates that people lived in this place as early as A.D. 900. The actual city was founded in 1531, and it is one of the oldest cities in Mexico. It has a cathedral that was built in the 1700s. While the city is modern and urban, hunting and fishing are nearby in the rural areas. This makes it an attractive place to live.

To the north of Culiacan is the state of Sonora. Sandwiched between the foothills and the bay, Guaymas is Sonora's largest port. The city dates back to a 1701 mission settlement. The United States invaded the city during the Mexican-American War, and the French occupied the city in the 1860s. Today this community of 130,000 people is growing. It doesn't compete with the large resorts, but it does offer beautiful beaches and a wide variety of water sports. Guaymas is the commercial side of the city, while San Carlos is developing a tourist area. Diving nearby shipwrecks is a popular attraction. Hollywood used Guaymas-San Carlos to film the 1998 movie *Zorro*.

The capital of Sonora, Hermosillo, was named after a general in the war with Spain for independence. This city is industrialized and modern, with a population of over 600,000. Like most of this region, this city is one of contrast. Surrounded by cattle and agricultural products, it also houses a large Ford plant and is a ranching supply center as well. The shops are filled with hats, boots, and other supplies needed by the cowboys who have been a part of Mexico for centuries. This city is prosperous, and it uses part of this prosperity to support Cuidad de Los Niños. This is a children's village built for the abandoned and abused children of Mexico. Some students from the University of Sonora built the first house for children in 1982, and the village now has 22 houses, a library, and classrooms.

CHRONOLOGY

1200 B.C.	Cochimi Indians live in Baja California
100 B.C.– A.D. 1300	Ancient native Mexicans paint petroglyphs in the caves of the Baja Peninsula.
900s	Indians live in Culiacan, Sinaloa.
1500s	The Spanish arrive in Mexico.
1600s	The Yaqui Indians make a treaty with the Spanish; the Seri Indians revolt.
1700s	Cora Indians revolt, and Spain sends the military to conquer them; Nueva Viscaya and Nueva Galicia are set up to govern this territory; the Jesuits are expelled.
1800s	Mexican independence is achieved; the French invade and then the Americans; Mexico gives up territory to the United States; North Pacific area is still isolated and largely undeveloped; the Seri are reduced to only 500 people; pearls are found at La Paz in Baja California Sur.
1900s	The Mexican Revolution occurs; irrigation projects aid agriculture, and other presidents continue to help develop the region; the Border Industrialization program precedes NAFTA, and the PAN political party wins support in the region.
2000	Vicente Fox, a PAN candidate, is elected president and chooses an assistant from the Pacific North.
2001	Mexico puts more focus on the Pacific North region as its population increases.
2002	Vicente Fox and other Latin American leaders attend conference in Argentina.

FOR MORE INFORMATION

BAJA CALIFORNIA

Government of Baja California
http://www.baja.gob.mx

State Tourism Office
Blvd. Díaz Ordaz s/n
Edif. Plaza Patria Nivel 3
CP 22400 Tijuana, B.C.
Tel: (66) 34-6330
Fax: (66) 34-3085
E-mail: dirpromocion@icanet.com.mx

BAJA CALIFORNIA SUR

Government of Baja California Sur
http://www.gbcs.gob.mx

State Tourism Office
Carr. Al Norte Km. 5.5 Fracc. Fidepaz
CP 23090 La Paz, B.C.S.
Tel: (112) 4-0100
Fax: (112) 4-0722
E-mail: turismo@lapaz.cromwell
        .com.mx

NAYARIT

Government of Nayarit
http://www.nayarit.gob.mx

Secretary of Tourism
E-mail: turnay3@tepic.megared.net.mx

State Tourism Office
Calz. del Ejército y Av. México s/n

Ex-Convento de la Cruz de Zacate
CP 63168 Tepic, Nay.
Tel: (32) 14-8071
Fax: (32) 14-1017

SINALOA

Government of Sinaloa
http://www.sinaloa.gob.mx

Sinaloa Development Council
phone: (67) 12-8232
fax: (67) 15-3459
E-mail: sinaloa@sinaloa-mex.org.mx

State Tourism Office
Av. Camarón Sabalo esq. Tiburon
Edificio Banrural 4 Piso
CP 82100 Mazatlán, Sin.
Tel: (69) 16-5160
Fax: (69) 16-5166

SONORA

Government of Sonora
http://www.sonora.gob.mx

State Tourism Office
Centro de Gobierno, Edif. Estatal
Norte 3er Nivel
Comonfort y Paseo Río
CP 83280 Hermosillo, Son.
Tel: (62) 17-0076
Fax: (62) 17-0076

57

GLOSSARY

Arid	A very dry region.
Canneries	Factories where canned foods are produced.
Duties	A tax on goods coming into the country.
Ejido system	A program in Mexico where the government sets aside farmland for communities; the land is owned in common and passed down from generation to generation.
Endangered	At risk of becoming extinct.
Exported	Shipped out of a country.
Fiestas	Mexican parties or celebrations.
Graphite	A soft black form of carbon that is used in lead pencils, electrolytic anodes, and nuclear reactors.
Habitat	The place or residence where a person, plant, or animal typically lives.
Imported	Shipped into a country.
Inlets	A small bay of water.
Interest rates	The percentages at which money is added to banked or borrowed money.
Irrigation	To bring a supply of water to a dry area in order to help crops grow.
Ironwood	A tough, hard wood.
Lagoons	A shallow sound or pond that leads into the ocean.
Lent	The 40 days before Easter; a time of fasting and thinking about sins.

Maquiladoras	Factories created to attract foreign business to Mexico by allowing them to do business cheaply.
Mestizo	A mix of Native American and European.
Migrating	Traveling from one area to another in search of warmer temperatures.
Mission	A group of people sent by a church to spread their faith or do social work.
Nomads	People who roam the land without a permanent home.
Petroglyphs	Rock paintings.
Prohibition	A policy in the United States that forbade the manufacture, sale, and transport of alcoholic beverages.
Reclamation	A program to take back farmland or other land from industrial or other uses.

THINGS TO DO AND SEE

BAJA CALIFORNIA NORTE
Tijuana's bullfighting rings
Jai alai arena in Tijuana
Mexitlan Park in Tijuana: 200 scale models of Mexico's most famous sites

BAJA CALIFORNIA SUR
Whale watching at Guerro Negro
Cabo San Lucas and La Paz beaches

SONORA
San Carlos beach resort
Expo Obregon: amusement park and cultural exposition
Pinacate Biosphere: volcanic park

SINALOA
Archeological museum in Mazatlán

NAYARIT
Beaches in Miramar, Santa Cruz, and Los Cocos
Tepic museums
Convent of La Cruz de Zacate
Isla Isabel nature preserve

FURTHER READING

Collis, John and David M. Jones (Eds.). *Blue Guide Mexico*. New York: Norton, 1997.

Gerhard, Peter. *The North Frontier of New Spain*. Norman: University of Oklahoma Press, 1993.

Larson, Peggy and Lane Larson. *The Deserts of the Southwest*. San Francisco: Sierra Club Books, 1997.

Mexico Travel Book. Tampa, Fla.: AAA Publishing, 2000.

Wilcock, John, Kal Muller, and Martha Ellen Zenfell (Eds.). *Insight Guides, Mexico*. New York: Langenscheidt Publishers, 1998

INTERNET RESOURCES

Baja Highway: The Catavina Desert
http://www.cababob.baja.com

INEGI (Geographic, Demographic, and Economic Information of Mexico)
http://www.inegi.gob.mx/diffusion/ingles/portadai.html

Mission Churches of the Sonoran Desert
http://www.dizzy.library.arizona.edu.

The Seri Indians of Sonora, Mexico
http://www.uapress.arizona.edu/online.bks/seris/history.htm

Tour by Mexico
http://www.tourbymexico.com

INDEX

PICTURE CREDITS

CONTRIBUTORS

Roger E. Hernández is the most widely syndicated columnist writing on Hispanic issues in the United States. His weekly column, distributed by King Features, appears in some 40 newspapers across the country, including the *Washington Post*, *Los Angeles Daily News*, *Dallas Morning News*, *Arizona Republic*, *Rocky Mountain News* in Denver, *El Paso Times*, and *Hartford Courant*. He is also the author of *Cubans in America*, an illustrated history of the Cuban presence in what is now the United States, from the early colonists in 16th-century Florida to today's Castro-era exiles. The book was designed to accompany a PBS documentary of the same title.

Hernández's articles and essays have been published in the *New York Times*, *New Jersey Monthly*, *Reader's Digest*, and *Vista Magazine*; he is a frequent guest on television and radio political talk shows, and often travels the country to lecture on his topic of expertise. Currently, he is teaching journalism and English composition at the New Jersey Institute of Technology in Newark, where he holds the position of writer-in-residence. He is also a member of the adjunct faculty at Rutgers University.

Hernández left Cuba with his parents at the age of nine. After living in Spain for a year, the family settled in Union City, New Jersey, where Hernandez grew up. He attended Rutgers University, where he earned a BA in Journalism in 1977; after graduation, he worked in television news before moving to print journalism in 1983. He lives with his wife and two children in Upper Montclair, New Jersey.

Janet Burt is a freelance writer. This is her first book for Mason Crest.